Choosing the Lake

Choosing the Lake

Poems by

Nina Clements

© 2024 Nina Clements. All rights reserved.
This material may not be reproduced in any form, published,
reprinted, recorded, performed, broadcast,
rewritten or redistributed without
the explicit permission of Nina Clements.
All such actions are strictly prohibited by law.

Cover design by Shay Culligan
Cover image "Stepping from Ice to Water" by Karl Stevens
Author photo by Maria Francesca Drews

ISBN: 978-1-63980-526-6

Kelsay Books
502 South 1040 East, A-119
American Fork, Utah 84003
Kelsaybooks.com

For Seth

Author's Note

Choosing the Lake is grounded in place, and that place is Madison, Wisconsin, where I fled after California. I had the good fortune of landing in a historic building downtown called The Bellevue. It is a red-brick building built in 1913–1914 with a courtyard garden, built-in bookshelves with leaded glass doors, beautiful hardwood floors, and lots of light. I rented it sight unseen from California. The owner told me on the phone that my apartment had "a partial lake view" of Lake Monona. I had never heard of it. I knew it was not the ocean, and I did not think of it again until I arrived. This partial lake view became everything, and my life became organized around my daily walk along the lake. I sat at my table in the sunroom, inside my box of windows, and I looked at the lake. I looked at the lake, and I wrote these poems.

Acknowledgments

Thank you to the following places, in which versions of these poems previously appeared:

Thimble Literary Magazine: "Lost"

Vox Populi: "Singing Bowl Massage"

Wild Roof Journal: "For Lisa, June 30"

"Final Lake" also appears in a festschrift for David Baker.

I would like to thank some of the many people who made the publication of this book possible. I'm grateful to my California and Madison poetry groups, who read many of these poems individually and as a manuscript. I'm so thankful for your compassion and precision as you held these poems. I'm grateful to Karl Stevens for reading the book and for believing in it so strongly that he insisted I send it out, specifically to Kelsay Books. I'm so glad I did! I am grateful to Jason Irwin for his continued encouragement and support of my work and for his careful reading. I am grateful to Marsha de la O for many reasons, especially for her reactions to the final poem in this book. Thank you. And I am, of course, grateful to Seth, who read the manuscript again and again.

Contents

I. First Encounters

Lakeview Apartment	17
Nighttime	18
Seagulls	19
October Lake	20
Precarious Steps	21
The Tender Side	22
Great Lake	23
Slow Exit	24
Lakeside Walk	25
Quarantine Lake	26
Stones	27
Dream, Your Sister	28
Thaw	29

II. Auditioner

The Auditioner	33
The First Audition	34
Falling In	35
The Auditioner Decides	36
Fall	37
Equanimity	38

III. Transition

That Kind of Woman	41
Lost	42
Devil's Lake	43
Tandem	44
Thanksgiving Lake	45
Christmas Vacation	46

IV. Seth

Prelude to Winter	49
Illicit at Midlife	50
Singing Bowl Massage	51
Choosing the Lake	52
No One Will Ever Love You	53
Bodies of Water	54
Diagnosis	55
Scar Tissue	56
Frozen Lake, January	57
Ice Lantern Festival	58
Continuously Variable Transmission	60
Spring	61
Gray Ice	62
The Heart	63
Clutch	64
Seth's Window	65
Moving	66
Your Sister and the Lake	67

V. Stillness

In Your Novel	71
Freedom	72
For Lisa, June 30	73
Mummy	74
Loneliness	75
Failed Scholar	76
Three Years of Lake View	77
Longing	78
Final Lake	79
We Walked on Water	80

I. First Encounters

Lakeview Apartment

Through a screen
of trees, it's there:
the lake in a city

your friends
can't remember.
Where have you

disappeared to? It's the lake,
the music on your phone,
that keeps you here, quiet.

Touching fingers to screen
at dusk—still too bright
for the light. The water moves,

flows and flutters for the birds.
These men will
never answer you.

But the breeze! You know
it's not the sea,
but Autumn is here,

another year
in which you will not
write your novel. This cold

is not California, two thousand
miles, but farther.
This loneliness takes

your breath. You chose
to leave, they say.
You chose the lake.

Nighttime

Push out the poison
into the toilet. So much
pressure. Not a baby,

but. Somehow you're still
a woman, even in the middle
of the night, when the lake

is only a dark cloud outside
your window. When you go
into the lake, the cold water

pours over your head,
and you think, the pollution.
The water foams

at your mouth. You want
something in your life
to be pure, to be yours,

but it is not this water.
It is not what you left
in the toilet.

Seagulls

You walked next
to the lake, and the seagulls
flew at your shoulders.
They don't know
it's not the ocean,
the vastness you left.
The sky was bright
blue, and the sun caught
the water, blinding silver.
Seagulls eat trash
but still manage majestic.

October Lake

The day begins gray,
no pink above the lake.
Just trees in the distance

that have begun to shed
their leaves. Your love
is tiring of you, or

are you tiring of him, or
has love itself become
a tired thing?

Precarious Steps

In the forest,
you both stood
on a plank bridge
and looked up—the light
was green through the leaves.
Every step became
delicate. You lived
in separate cities.
He had never seen
the ocean. You came together
weekly to walk near
a lake, this time
in a forest. There was always
a beginning and end
to your time together.
You trampled the dead leaves
and stared at the shafts
of light dancing on your faces.

The Tender Side

The tenderness of light
in the morning
through the thinning

leaves of the soon-
to-be-bare trees.
How gently it reaches

your window and shines
upon the belly
of a cat.

Great Lake

You drove east to the great
lake where there was sand,
a breeze, waves. Not an ocean,
but close enough. Sun pricked
the rocks, and you filled your pockets
with new shapes and colors.
You could almost forget
the impossible vastness
of the ocean. The salt
hanging in the air. Here
you are now, a Midwesterner.
Later, you brought sand
into the bed. That part
was the same.

Slow Exit

You walk together
along the lake
but see nothing.
You don't see
the ducks treading water
in perfect pairs.
Soon, he will leave you
to the pandemic.
How will it feel
to walk alone?

Lakeside Walk

You walked the gravel alone
today and looked
for the goslings.
They're bigger and browner;
the downy yellow you so admired
is gone. The clouds
are gray here, and so
is the lake. The same gray
as when he carried your breakfast
on your favorite blue
China plate. Staring
through the window
at the water, you ate.

Quarantine Lake

The city has come outside
to stare at the dark water,
darker than the storm's sky.

People mask their mouths,
exercise the appearance
of freedom, moving muscles fast,
faster than you ever will.

Stones

Stillness beneath the moving water:
the stones rest at the bottom
of the lake, visible from water's edge.
Each flat stone, an intention.
The intention of the mother to bear
you for your entire life.
She is like other animals in this way:
she raised her young and set them free.
Others might say: she cast them out.

Dream, Your Sister

In the dream, your sister
took the knife from your hand
and sliced the snake's
head away. Gone,
it was gone. The beating
of your heart woke
you. The lake was a still,
frozen disc, dusted
with snow. She's always
saving you.

Thaw

The crust of white
has given way to blue
movement, right
to left, west to east.
But your heart doesn't
yet know it is spring.

II. Auditioner

The Auditioner

The Auditioner has a kind
face but is not kind. The lake
is dark between the dwindling
leaves. It's early for such darkness,
yet you know this night
will swallow you whole, digest
you through the belly of a snake
until the sun comes again.

The First Audition

He tells you, you have many
fine qualities after
one date. You sat next
to each other only a handful
of hours, but he has seen
many fine qualities
deep in your dark eyes,
coming up and out of your pores
like sweat. It's only the first
audition. You consider the lake,
the wind on your shoulders.
One of the lake's many fine qualities.

Falling In

You slipped into the lake
like a fish, but clumsy.
The waves at the rocks
were too much
for your balance.
He fell into you
with such ease,
his tongue squirming
in your mouth.
But he was no better
than the lake—rough
and unsteadying.
Where is your equanimity?
With the rocks at the bottom.

The Auditioner Decides

You're eccentric in all the right
ways, he tells you over
the phone, as he rattles
off your "fine qualities."
Cool as hell, as well, one
in a million. You stare
at the silver lake
through the window.
Thank you for taking
my call, he says. Such
a nice, Midwestern man.

Fall

No one will save
you from the changing
of the seasons.
Summer turns over,
and the leaves yellow
like old paper, fall.
Soon, it will be bare
branches and the frozen lake.
How many ways
can he tell you
he doesn't want
to know you?

Equanimity

Walk along the river
between the two lakes,
the connector and through-
line. Stand at the center
of a bridge and look out.
You want it to be the end
of all wanting.

III. Transition

That Kind of Woman

You walk along the lake path
to the co-op, even though it is longer.
You are the kind of woman

who buys organic lemons at the co-op.
You are wearing a dress,
because you are the kind of woman

who wears dresses in summer, legs
bare to the breeze. So it should be
no surprise when the woman approaches

with her story, which might even be true,
because you look like the kind of woman
who gives her money away. She compliments

your dress, and then you realize you *are*
the kind of woman who gives her money away.
You have been playing a part so long;

you didn't realize you had become it.
The blue of the lake is the blue of your dress.

Lost

How could you have been so
careless? You have lost
your mother's love.

You thought you'd put it away
inside a dresser drawer, painted
pine. This was before

the lake in your window, before
the Midwest and its loneliness.
You were still in California.

Perhaps you lost it in the move,
or one of the cats ate it. Small
and round, a ball of amber.

Devil's Lake

So clear this lake,
not like yours.
The water is a mirror—

you can see it easily
from the top
of the mountain,

legs buzzing from the climb.
You are afraid of heights.
He puts his arm around you,

and your mind goes white.
There is only the lake
and his hand

on your shoulder—
the crowd vanishes.
His hand is warm,

solid as the ground.

Tandem

There's still this loneliness,
even riding on the tandem
bicycle, the lake a blur

of blue on the left.
You are too afraid to focus
your gaze on the geese

in the patch of sunlight.
You stare instead at the back
of the man in front of you,

the white, smooth scalp.
How tired you are,
of being afraid.

Afraid to ride a bicycle,
afraid to fall to the ground
and hurt yourself in some

irrevocable way. Afraid
to be with and without
a man.

Thanksgiving Lake

You walk east with the water.
The lake is flat gray
today. No sunlight, no salt
in the air like there was that year
in Plymouth, out on the jetty,
rocks piled high. You were married
then, happy in your sweaters.
The real rock was disappointing,
as if at the bottom of a well.
This time, you are alone,
and you can see the tops of rocks
peeking out from beneath the water's
surface, gray against gray.

Christmas Vacation

The man whispers
against your skin
that he loves you.

But he is going away.
He'll be far off
in another country

while you watch Christmas
movies with your sister.
The lake will be frozen

by the time
he returns.
Can love travel

in text messages across
time zones and the ocean?
You'll be here,

and he will be
in your imagination,
flashes of the sound

of his accent, the grip
of his hand on your leg,
phantoms of feeling.

IV. Seth

Prelude to Winter

The edges near the sand
are gently frozen—clear
enough to see the rocks

underneath. It's too early
to walk across it, no snow.
Instead, you both trudge

through mud
around Indian Lake,
talking of home.

Long curly hair
frames his face against
blue sky.

He's a kind man
with dark eyes
that compel you

to keep walking.
He takes your hand
when you stumble;

he lifts you
from the mud.

Illicit at Midlife

There is a man
in your bed with more
hair than you.

The long, dark curls
feel good to pull
against the pillow.

His mouth in the curve
where neck meets shoulder,
his fingers making slow

circles at your center.
You belong to someone else,
but here is your lover.

Dark curls mixed with gray,
there is no pretense
of youth. You know what

you are doing.
Lines beneath dark eyes.
He does, too.

You think, though,
you might get to keep
each other in the bed

for a long while.

Singing Bowl Massage

For Carolin

She places the bowls
on your body—
the heart and belly,
deep breaths
rise and fall.
You are on the table
but also floating
in the center
of a lake. Vibrations
at your core.
The table begins to shake.

She turns you over, gently,
positions your head
lower than your body.
Arms hang down, and bowls sing
on your shoulders, where the tension
hides. Bowls along your spine,
and the chiming of the gong,
the singing song of vibration
in your body. You feel it then—
trying to crawl up your throat,
out your mouth, a cough.
Get the men out, it says.

You want the calm
of the lake
as you walk along
its edge. *Get the men
out,* you say again.
Get out. Get out.

Alone in your body,
the water placid, only
the slight vibration
of the heart.

Choosing the Lake

You left the salt and shame
in California. Each man
a grain of sand in your bed.

How it itched.
Now you choose
fresh water,

the strip of land
between lakes,
the plate glass

that lets you peer
through bare branches
down to water.

How the wind burns
each winter, chafes
your skin pink and clean.

No One Will Ever Love You

No one will ever love you
like the mother from whose body
you crawled.

Your fingers are her fingers;
the line of your throat belongs
to her. She was unconscious

and could not feel your heart's
first beatings. You grew
to know the heat of her hand,

the slap from her memories.
How it stung.
Now, the blue water

protects you
from her, the sound
of waves in your ears.

Bodies of Water

Your first sand was Lake Erie's.
You hated how it scrubbed your tender feet.
There wasn't much money,
and the lake wasn't far.
Later, there were trips
to the ocean, family
beaches in humid South Carolina.
The relentless roar of waves
rolling in and out without pause.
Your parents beached themselves
in the sand, worn out. You wanted
more excitement—
theater, museums, culture.
All they could manage was sitting
before the waves.
What better symphony,
you thought, years later.

Diagnosis

In the fifteen months before
your sister came, you were a ball
without consciousness. You only
remember the world with her
in it. When she touched the earth
with her chubby fingers, you gripped
the dirt in her strong little hand.
You were alone in the womb,
alone in the water. How will it feel
to be alone in the world?

Scar Tissue

For Greg

The hypnotist tells
you to shift, change,
release. Clear the damage
away. Tomorrow, you will
walk on the frozen
lake. They're afraid
for you, back home.
Scar tissue along the seams
of the heart like ridges
of ice, tectonic plates
coming together and pulling
apart. There's no danger,
you tell them. People walk
across all the time.
You want to tell them
to shift, change, release
their fear, but it's the only
love they can show.

Frozen Lake, January

You walk together on frozen water,
gloves nearly touching. You don't speak a word,
mouths covered in cloth, glasses fogged over.
They've planted a forest of Christmas trees
on the lake. You breathe heavily
with the effort of forging a path through
white, untouched inches; you remove your mask
and see others there who have braved the cold.
All together, marveling at the strips
of cloth tied to branches. New wishes for
the new year. You look to Seth, see
his lips crack into a smile, the flesh chapped.

Ice Lantern Festival

I.

You know nothing
of the festival,
but you have left the frozen
lakes behind you
for the quilted countryside
of snow and red barns.
The sound of tires gripping
the sand in the road, snow
still coming down, the blast
of the heater. He is driving.
You are exchanging
your small city for a tiny town.
No one will know where you are.

II.

They line the sidewalks
with their flickering.
The best ones have flowers
and bits of pinecone frozen
into them. An upside down
bucket, empty in the center,
for the candle and its light.
The heat melts the top,
softens ice into shards
of glass. It is the closest
you have come to prayer
in a long while. You stand
there together, quiet except
for the flames of candles, the crunch
of snow as you step in place
to keep warm.

III.

After the lanterns, you
are silent; you lie
together in the bed, hips
and shoulders touching.
You wonder, *do I love
this man?* He glides
a finger down your arm.
His breath in your ear,
his heart beating below
your hand.

Continuously Variable Transmission

The car moves up the hill with only
a little groan. The transmission
continues. No control, he says,

not like a manual.
But you want it anyway.
You buy it anyway.

You want to drive the whole
way around the lake
while maintaining

the same speed.
You want to do it
alone, because you do not like

to drive men in your car.
The man in the car
doesn't matter.

The man in this car's dark
eyes search, scan the street
for danger that you're not

smart enough to see;
hands grip the door.
How like a reproach.

Spring

You're trapped
in your box of windows
waiting for branches
to bud with spring.
In the waking dream,
a scorpion but no sister
to save you. The water
moves and moves again.

Gray Ice

You miss the white,
the light. Months ago
it seems, the sun
shone on the ice
skaters setting out.
The doctor told
you everything is fine,
but why are you in Wisconsin?
You miss the heat
of California in February,
the sun so relentless there.

The Heart

The crust of ice around
your heart does not thaw
as the lake does. As a child,
your mother fed you pepperoni
and poison, taught you
to guard your heart.
It is time for the ice to melt,
to open to the breeze
and blossoms in the trees.
But it cannot. Her advice
has taken root in sheets of ice.
You walk alongside
the lake alone, as you always do.

Clutch

The way Seth grips
your shoulder. Hold onto me,
he says. His piano-playing
fingers are stronger than you
knew. He is all there is to cling to.
The cleaving and connecting
of skin, of limbs, the vise
of his left hand on your shoulder
and the scent of spring
through the open window.
The lake knows you are happy
and that you can't bear it.

Seth's Window

Moths and butterflies,
but no lake. Gravel
and railroad tracks,
but no lake. It is not
your window; it is not
your house. The need to see
that blue is drowning
you. But the lake of your loneliness
isn't here. Instead, the squirrels
careen from tree to tree.
Do you want your lover,
or do you want the lake?

Moving

There is one room
in his house for you.
Everything must fit.

You cannot bring
your window
with the lake. You must

exchange it
for the railroad tracks
and gravel, the flitting

of small birds
on the red feeder
hanging from the back fence.

Every book, every journal,
every album—the proof
of your life—must be contained

within a single room.
How small
you must become.

Your Sister and the Lake

Your sister has not seen
your lake, but her eyes
are ringed with brown,
like the shore. Those
dark circles, the discoloration
of the dead when the blood
pools in unnatural places.
Life is not endless;
you are in the middle of things.
The thought of outliving
her stutters your heart,
ripples in the water.

V. Stillness

In Your Novel

The lake ripples
through the window.
You were like a child

with whom no one
would play. That is to say,
you were hurting.

You wandered
the prairie alone
and did not know

your face
was lovely.
Everything was wrong.

He left you behind.
In the novel, you still
want to catch up.

Freedom

When Seth tells you
he will get the vasectomy—
that he will stop your monthly

anxiety with a minor
surgical procedure, painfully
reversible, because you asked him to—

you are holding hands.
In that moment,
with more certainty and force

than ever before,
he is proclaiming
his love to you;

also to the surgeon who will perform
the pulling and slicing; to his family
when he says, deliberately, there will be

no children; to your family, who now
know he will face the knife for you.
He will silence that yowling

uncertainty, the daily white pill.
You turn, keep walking
alongside the lake. The sun

sets, light
dances on the pools
of algae, metallic.

For Lisa, June 30

Algae swirls on the surface of the lake,
the smell of rot in your nose.
Another year and you mark
your sister's birth as June fades
away. Whorls of ink cover
her skin, large holes divide
her earlobes. She redrew
herself, but she is still
your mother's daughter. Still her
depression and mania, never slow
and steady. As a baby, she screamed
whenever her tender
feet touched sand.

Mummy

He said, Come sit next to Mummy,
darling, and pounded the cushion, raising
dust. He handed you a gin and tonic,
limes always on the counter. Your own
mother had never been this kind, so steadily.
Every day, a greeting. The loveseat, white,
was too small for him but you squeezed together,
always watching something on the small television,
a film, or more likely, *The Sopranos,* which gave
you nightmares. You hid your face in Jake's armpit
to block out the violence. The clink of ice
cubes in a glass, the smell of lime.
Now, you sit and watch the lake, alone.

Loneliness

You walk into the sea
with Seth, up to your waist
in the Atlantic's bathwater.

He keeps walking
until water sluices down
his shoulders. Salt

in abundance. How it coats
and thickens your hair,
the grit it leaves on your skin.

Now, you miss the lake, blooms
of untouchable algae.
You are alone as you walk

back to your spot in the sand,
so different from your ambles
together along the lake.

How strange to be lonely in this crush
of bodies in the sun, voices
louder than the ocean.

Failed Scholar

Look at yourself, here
in your room, your box
of windows above

blue water. The sun rises,
and the lake reflects
the sun back to the sun—

glimmers, until there are spots
in your vision. You are still
in the Midwest, trapped

in the circle of the lake
by your conventional need
for the steady

paycheck, health insurance.
You are wasting
your life, author of nothing.

You spend your time searching
for the books of others—
a penance

for your sins, the pride
and ambition that once filled
you, bloated as an old sausage.

Three Years of Lake View

Some nights, a purple smudge
above the water.
Every day, this tightening

of your chest, this holding
of your breath,
this hard clench.

The sky lightens,
almost brightens, then stops.
The water throbs

gently. You are facing
yourself in the Midwest.
You are facing the lake.

Longing

Always something that's not here—
the jasmine along the sidewalks
in California; the way that man
with words etched along his body
kissed you, said *my sweat
on your lips*. The scent of rosemary;
the basket of dirty vegetables
from the farmer's market.
Pour the memories onto the table.
Sift and sort. Take only
the most tender for your plate.

Final Lake

For David Baker

You woke up wrong; the lake
was gone. It was yours
for a time, through

the corner window, smallest
glimpse until you turned
your head. Then it was all

blue water and sky, the green
locust tree a screen between
you and the shimmering water.

How lonely you were when you
first discovered its depths.
Now you are gone

from it, waking each day
in a blue room with your lover.
You didn't know it was the final

lake the day you left. You thought
to return one last time after
you made the wood shine, left

the bathroom bright, clean. You
took your last look but didn't know.
Now you imagine the final glance,

your fingers pressed to the window.
You know that even this
love can be taken from you.

We Walked on Water

We went back to the lake
in January, walked onto ice
near the hockey players
and held chapped hands.
Through sage smoke
and ringing bowls,
we spoke our poems,
pledged ourselves:
each to each. The sun
came upon us as we slid
the rings onto stiff fingers.
You are my home, we said.
This is our lake.

About the Author

Nina Clements earned an MFA from Sarah Lawrence College. She is the author of the chapbook *Set the Table* and the poetry collection *Our Mother of Sorrows*. Her poems have appeared in *Bellevue Literary Review, Spillway, Prairie Schooner,* and other places. Originally from Pittsburgh, she now lives in Madison, Wisconsin.

www.ingramcontent.com/pod-product-compliance
Lightning Source LLC
Chambersburg PA
CBHW030911170426
43193CB00009BA/815